I Knew When I Was Five
an illustrated book about our natural compassion

by Anne Mitchell
illustrated by Suzanne King

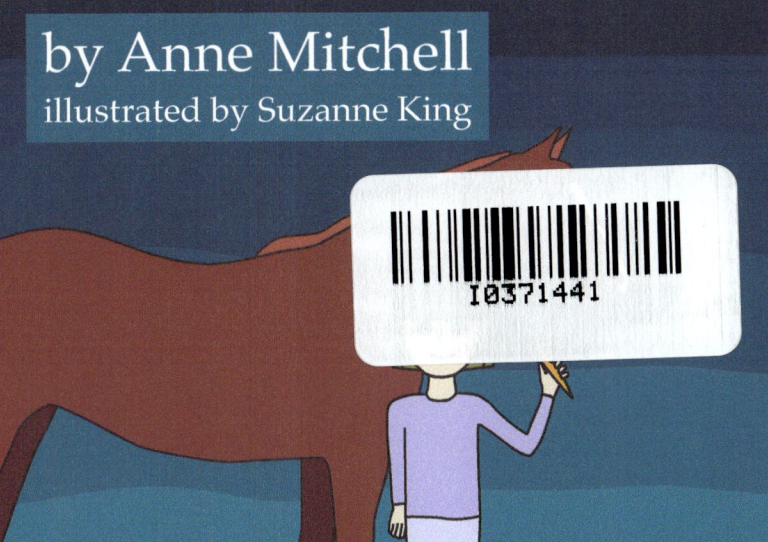

This book is dedicated secondly to Doris Abrams, the only adult in my childhood who nurtured my compassion and empathy and who shared Flint with me. And first to Flint—the big, goofy, chestnut Thoroughbred I fell in love with at first sight when I was seven—who lived in Doris's barn. You always treated me like a peer, took me seriously, taught me everything, and loved me fully. It was such a joy and honor to be your friend. I did learn your lessons, it just took me a long time to develop the courage to live them. I am forever grateful. - Anne Mitchell

The illustrations in this book are dedicated to the child in each of us. - Suzanne King

Praise for
I KNEW WHEN I WAS FIVE

" Anne's book will help readers truly relate to an array of animals that our society too often views as food, not fellow creatures worthy of living out their lives in peace. *I Knew When I Was Five* will motivate readers to rethink their food choices and explore how to live in a way that is more compassionate to animals, people, and our planet. "

— Jesse Kharbanda, Executive Director,
Hoosier Environmental Council

" This charming and thought-provoking book is a must-read for children of all ages! It will empower them to foster their innate compassion for animals and consider how their everyday actions affect our fellow earthlings. If every child were to do that, the world would be such a better place! "

— Wendy Eikenberry, animal rights advocate

" We wish we had read *I Knew When I Was Five* when we were five! It's a beautiful book that can lead to healthier childhoods and richer, more meaningful lives! "

— Joanna Samorow-Merzer, artist &
Glen Merzer, author, *Own Your Health*

Copyright © 2021 by Anne Mitchell.
All rights reserved. No portion of this book, except for brief review, may be reproduced, stored in a retrieval system, or transmitted in any form or by any means — electronic, mechanical, photocopying, recording, or otherwise — without the written permission of the author.

Author: Anne Mitchell
Illustrator: Suzanne King

ISBN-13: 978-1-7374438-0-3
Library of Congress Control Number: 2021912274

Published by:
Game B Press
Speedway, Indiana, USA
gamebpress.com

I knew when I was five
and no one had to tell me.

That killing is wrong.

Lobsters have complex lives.

The women choose
whose babies they will have and
mothers carry their eggs
for 9 to 11 months
before they are born.

Lobsters grow old
and wise
and can live 100 years
and grow 3 feet long
and weigh 40 pounds.

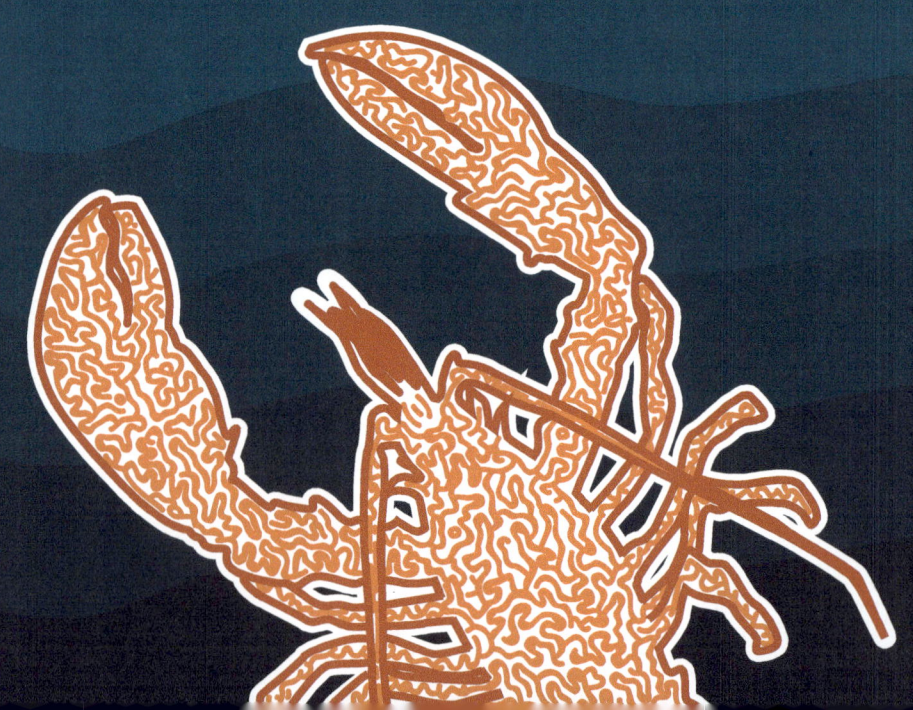

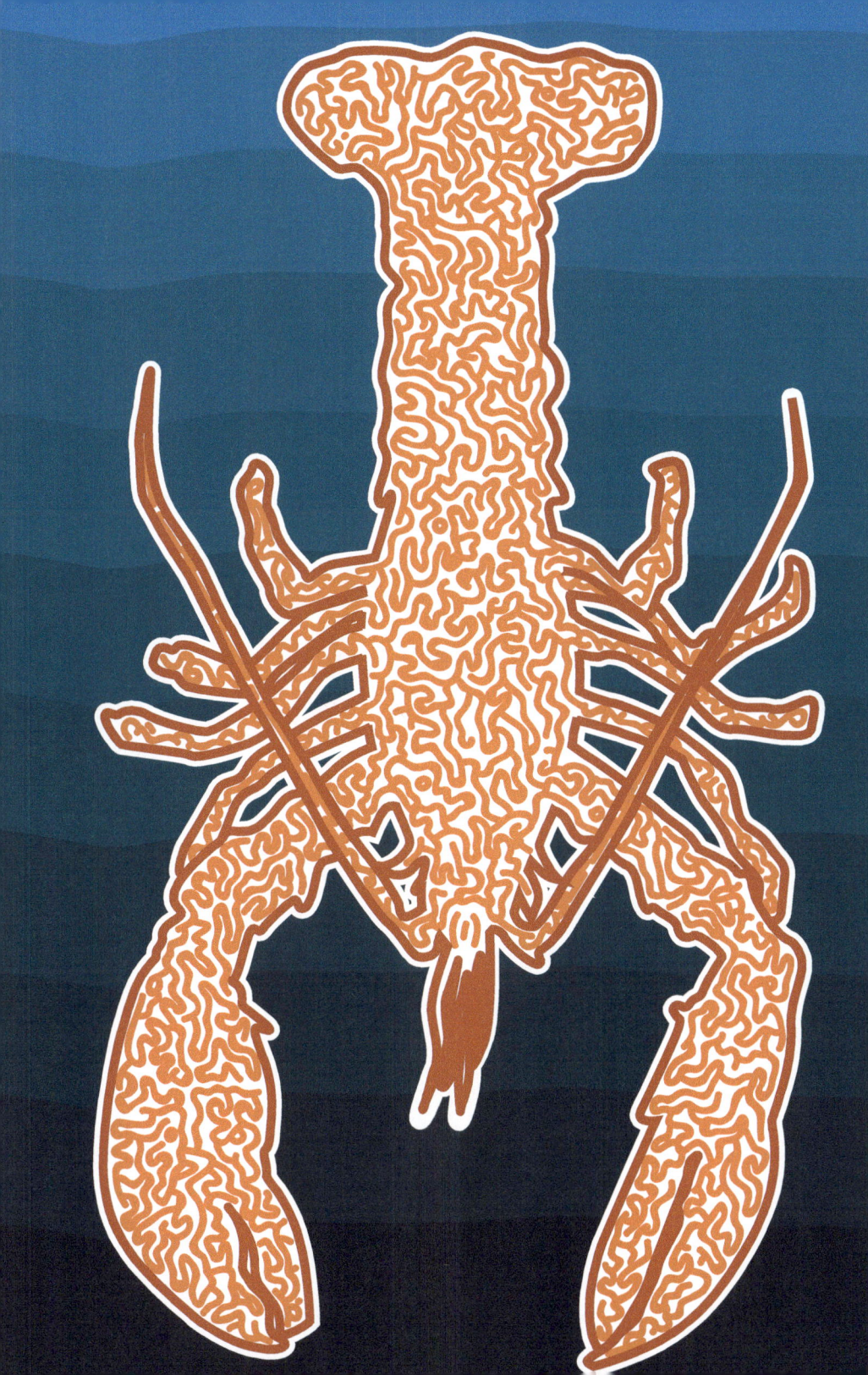

I knew when I was five
and no one had to tell me

that boiling a 1-pound,
5-year-old lobster
alive
to satisfy human tastebuds

was wrong.

Rabbits are gregarious
and live in communities
of up to 100 individuals.

They build houses
underground together
with separate rooms
for living and sleeping

and make lifelong friends
who play together,
calm each other
when stressed,
and nurture each other
when sick.

I knew when I was eight
and no one had to tell me

that killing and skinning
40 rabbits
so that one human
can wear a fur coat

was wrong.

Chickens are proud
and inquisitive
and live in large,
stable social groups.

They feel joy and fear
and are very curious.

Chickens are good mothers
whose wings
protect their babies.

I knew when I was twelve
and no one had to tell me

that killing and cooking
the chickens
from next door

— the very individuals who
came through the fence
to play with my horse —

was wrong.

Cows are gentle giants,
contemplative, collaborative
and compassionate.

They form lifelong friendships,
enjoy intellectual challenges,
and jump for joy
when they solve a problem.

I knew when I was sixteen
and no had to tell me

that making friends with a calf
— playing with her,
caring for her,
bathing and grooming her
for the 4-H show —
only to kill her,
dismember her,
and eat her

was wrong.

Pigs are smart enough
to play video games
against chimpanzees
and win.

Pigs are peaceful,
rarely show anger,
and are very kind
to each other.

I knew when I was twenty
and no one had to tell me

that "celebrating"
with co-workers
while a teenage pig with
an apple wedged in his mouth
roasted over an open fire
to please our palates

was wrong.

Deer are highly social beings, with women living communally, caring for their infants and children.

Groups of teenage boys hang out together, finding food and staying safe.

The men are territorial and live a more solitary life.

I knew when I was thirty-two
and no one had to tell me

that stalking, baiting,
and shooting unarmed deer
for fun

was wrong.

But someone did
have to point out —
even though I
disapproved of hunting,
finding it cruel and unnecessary,
every individual deer
had a chance to outrun
the arrow or the bullet

while not a single cow or pig or chicken ever had a chance against the slaughterhouse blade.

I knew when I was five
and no one had to tell me.

I knew when I was eight
and no one had to tell me.

I knew when I was twelve
and no one had to tell me.

I knew when I was sixteen
and no one had to tell me.

I knew when I was twenty
and no one had to tell me.

**I knew when I was thirty-two.
And yet...**

the confinement
the torture
the killing
the eating

of sentient beings continues

with numbers so large
they are incomprehensible;
70 BILLION land animals
a year.

More animals die
for human food
each week
than all the humans killed
in all the wars
in all of recorded history.

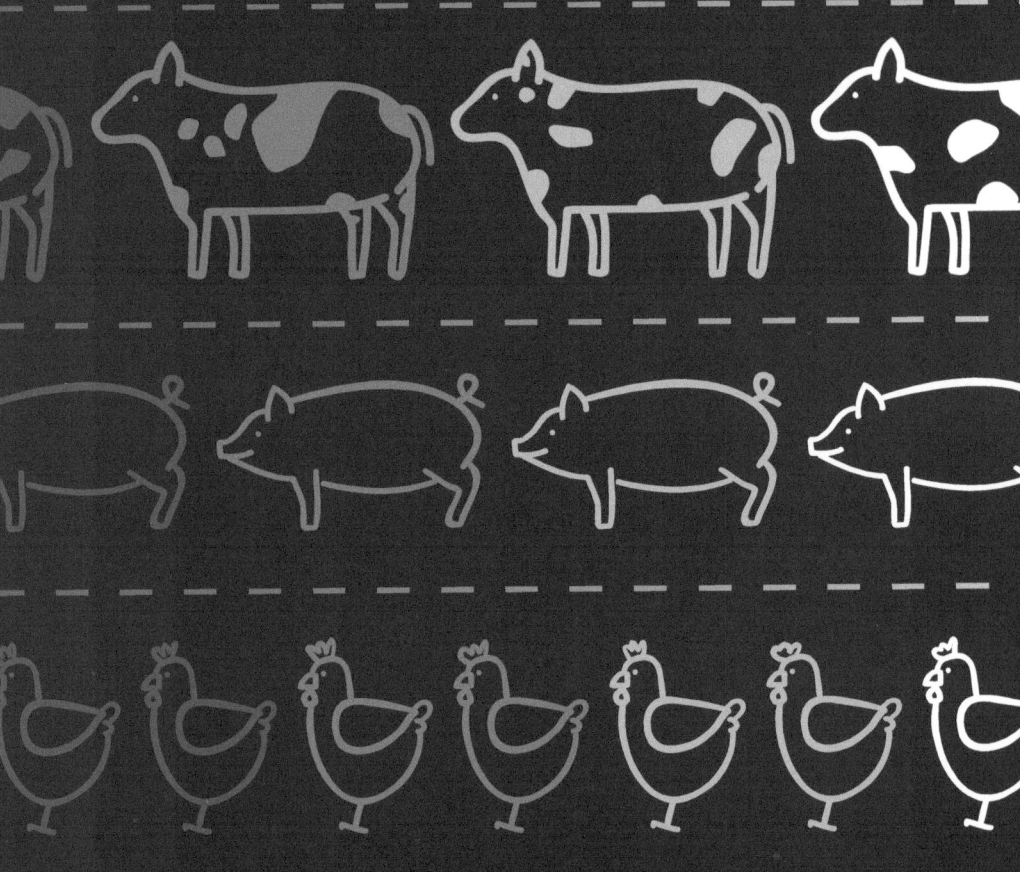

When will we all know enough to stop?

And when will the adults
support the children
who already know?

Questions to consider:

For children:

1) Are there things in your life that you've known are "wrong" like the girl in the book?

2) What would have helped you in those situations? What would you like an adult to do in those situations?

3) What animals do you see where you live? What animals do you like learning about?

For adults:

1) How do the children in your life show their compassion? How do they learn about issues like discrimination & violence?

2) How can you better support the children in your life? What do they love doing? (If you don't know, ask them!)

3) When you were a child, did you know some things you saw were "wrong" too? Did you have an adult to help you?

Actions to consider:

1) With the help of an adult, share your answer to Question 1 with us and other children at: gamebpress.com

2) Do something for a sibling, friend, or other animal to help or support them. What would be helpful for them?

3) Use the following pages to draw any images that come to mind when thinking about Question 3. (And consider taking a photo to share with us at gamebpress.com)

1) When spending time with a child, be present. (Consider this when spending time with anyone—especially children.)

2) When a child in your life asks you a question, find a way to tell "the truth." Consider the lies that society expects us to tell our children and the cycles you can help break.

3) For the birthday of a child in your life, help them gift a present to someone else—someone who appears to not "deserve" it.

Draw your own page of the book!

Name: Date:

Compassion IS possible

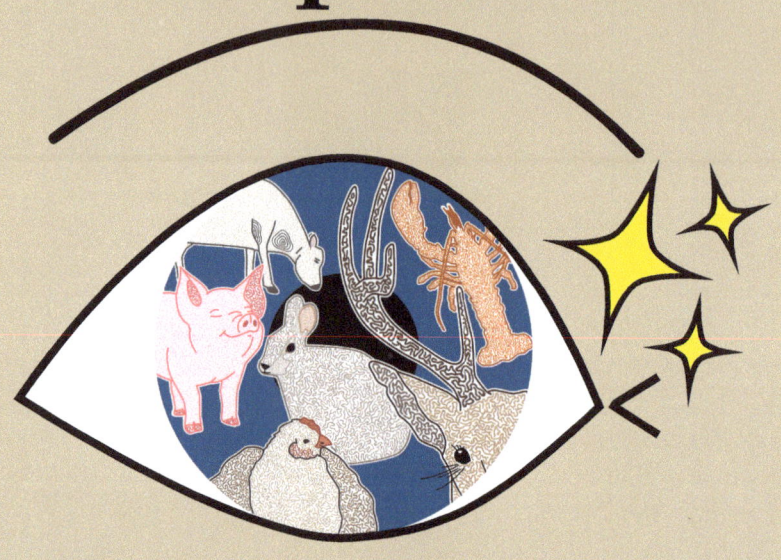

and here are some resources to get there.

Resources & Support:

Other Books

- The Vegucated Family Table: Irresistable Vegan Recipes and Proven Tips for Feeding Plant-Powered Babies, Toddlers, and Kids
  by Marisa Miller Wolfson and Laura Delhaur
- Disease-Proof Your Child: Feeding Kids Right
  by Dr. Joel Fuhrman
- Nourish: The Definitive Plant Based Nutrition Guide for Families
  by Dr. Reshma Shah and Brenda Davis, RD
- That's Why We Don't Eat Animals
  by Ruby Roth

Movies

- Okja
- Spirit: Stallion of the Cimarron
- Charlotte's Web

Websites

- PlantBasedPediatrician.com
- MyVeganChild.org
- PlantBasedJuniors.org
- BiteSizedVegan.org

More Praise for
I KNEW WHEN I WAS FIVE

" *I Knew When I Was Five* is a beautifully written and illustrated book that celebrates the innate compassion and respect that we all have for our fellow living beings that cohabit the earth.

It provides an important voice that cultivates and encourages kindness and empathy in children, rather than stifling it, as popular culture often does through messages of indifference toward fellow humans and non-human animals.

The questions and actions to consider provide an opportunity for caregivers to continue a dialogue to evoke the thoughts, emotions, and calls to action that will make compassion to all sentient beings a part of who they are and how they live. We look forward to sharing this book with our daughter and using it to launch a discussion about how we each can contribute to a kinder world. "

— Katelin Rupp, Co-Founder, Indy VegFest

> *I Knew When I Was Five* shares a powerful message and gives a glimpse into experiences many have had growing up in a culture that has normalized eating fellow animals. Kindness and compassion is what is most natural to us. We know at a deep intuitive level that harming fellow beings does not serve us. This book takes you on a journey of that inner knowing that is incredibly precious and important to tap into in order to create a more peaceful world.
>
> — Anna Ferguson, author, *World Peace Yoga*, and Founder, Heärt Montessori

---

> Anne has written a wonderful book that accurately conveys the individuality and sentience of the animals some people see as food.
>
> It is beautifully illustrated and my hope is that every adult will read it to a child in their life. That said, the message is important to those of all age groups.
>
> — Mark Pruitt, Co-Founder & VP, Uplands Peak Sanctuary

www.ingramcontent.com/pod-product-compliance
Lightning Source LLC
Chambersburg PA
CBHW042235090526
44589CB00001B/7